# Hello, Cats!

Storey Publishing

**Cats are frisky and fascinating creatures!** Whether you have a cat in your family or hope to someday, you can have fun discovering different kinds of cats, learning about cat behavior, and becoming friends with cats. In this book, you'll . . .

Discover cats of all shapes and sizes!

Meet curious kittens and fancy purebreds.

**FELINE** means "relating to cats."

Learn what cats mean when they meow or purr.

Find out about feline tails, ears, and eyes.

Watch a kitten grow.

Study a cat's behavior.

Keep a cat journal with stickers.

# Let's Be Friends

When you see a cat you don't know, don't rush up and pet her. Some cats are happy to say hello, but most cats like to make the first move, so be patient. Here are some ways to make friends with a new cat.

**1** Move slowly and quietly, so the cat won't be frightened. Sit still and let the cat come to you.

**2** Staring into a cat's eyes might scare her. Instead, look away or a little to one side of the cat.

**3** Cats use their noses to learn about people. Let a cat come up to you and have a sniff before you make a move.

**4** When the cat is near you, slowly extend your index finger for her to sniff. Many cats will rub their cheek on your finger. That's their way of shaking hands!

**5** Move your finger gently down her back. If the cat likes that, use your whole hand to pet her, always moving from head to tail.

# Frisky Kittens

Newborn kittens are like tiny balls of fur. Their mother feeds them milk, keeps them warm, and cleans them with her tongue. At first, kittens sleep most of the time, but after a few weeks, they are ready to play and explore!

A family of kittens is called a **LITTER**.

Young kittens have blue eyes that change to brown, green, or gold within 8 weeks.

Growing kittens need a lot of sleep.

Newborn kittens can't see or hear for the first week.

Kitten claws are tiny but very sharp!

Mama cats teach their kittens how to behave.

# WATCH A KITTEN GROW

Kittens are adorable, but they grow up fast! Within a year, they are fully grown. Take a look at how quickly this kitten grows up.

2 weeks old | 5 weeks old | 7 weeks old | 3 months old

## Life Stages

**Kitten (under 1 year)**
Kittens need a lot of sleep because when they are awake, they spend all their time bouncing around, exploring, and playing with anything that moves!

**Adult (1 to 12 years)**
After they grow out of the energetic kitten stage, most cats still love to play. If you are adopting an older cat, it is easier to observe the cat's personality.

**Senior cat (12+ years)**
As they age, cats slow down and sleep more. They might not be able to jump as high or be as active, but many still enjoy playing with toys.

4 months old

5 months old

1 year old

The oldest cat on record was Creme Puff, who lived to be 38 years old!

## A Cat's Age in Human Years

1 cat year = **15** human years

2 cat years = **24** human years

5 cat years = **36** human years

15 cat years = **76** human years

20 cat years = **96** human years

A **6-month-old kitten** is equal to a 10-year-old child!

# Black Cats

Cats can come in many different colors. The most common color is black. Have you ever seen one?

Many black cats have a little bit of white on them somewhere.

Most black cats have yellow eyes.

Tuxedo cats look like they are dressed up in a formal suit!

Gray is a mix of black and white hairs.

Most black cats are males.

## Lucky or Not?

In medieval England, black cats were associated with witchcraft. Some people still see them as unlucky. But in Japanese folklore and in ancient Egypt, people viewed black cats as symbols of good luck.

# Parts of a Cat

Sit quietly and look closely at the body of a cat. See if you can name all the different parts. Notice any parts that move or twitch. What do you think is the purpose of each part?

- ear
- eye
- nose
- whiskers
- back
- tail
- hock (ankle)
- paws
- elbow
- toes

A cat's nose pad has a unique pattern of ridges, like a person's fingerprint.

# WHAT DO CATS DO ALL DAY?

Cats are busy sleeping, playing, rubbing, scratching, pouncing, and using the litter box. Watch a cat and notice his behaviors. Why do you think he does each one?

Cats spend a lot of time cleaning themselves!

Cats sleep a lot—up to 18 hours a day!

Like wild cats, domestic cats like to hunt.

Cats are carnivores. They need meat to stay healthy.

Cats kick litter over their pee and poop to hide it.

Cats scratch to sharpen their claws, mark their territory, and let out their feelings.

Cats pounce on toys like prey!

# All About Tails

Tails help cats balance when they leap. Have you seen any tails with patterns or shapes like these?

Colorful

Feathery

Fluffy

Curled

Striped

Stubby

# Tails Talk

**Cats use their tails to communicate how they're feeling. The way a cat moves her tail can tell you a lot, if you know what to look for.**

Hello!

A tail that is straight up in the air means that a cat is happy to see you and wants to be friends.

I'm scared!

A cat with a puffed-up tail and an arched back is afraid. He is making himself look bigger and braver.

I'm mad.

Unlike a dog wagging a friendly tail, a cat lashes her tail rapidly back and forth to show anger or displeasure. Best to give her some time to cool down!

# White Cats

Pure white is one of the rarest cat colors. But there are many cats that are mostly white with a spot of color or a combination of white and another color. Take a look!

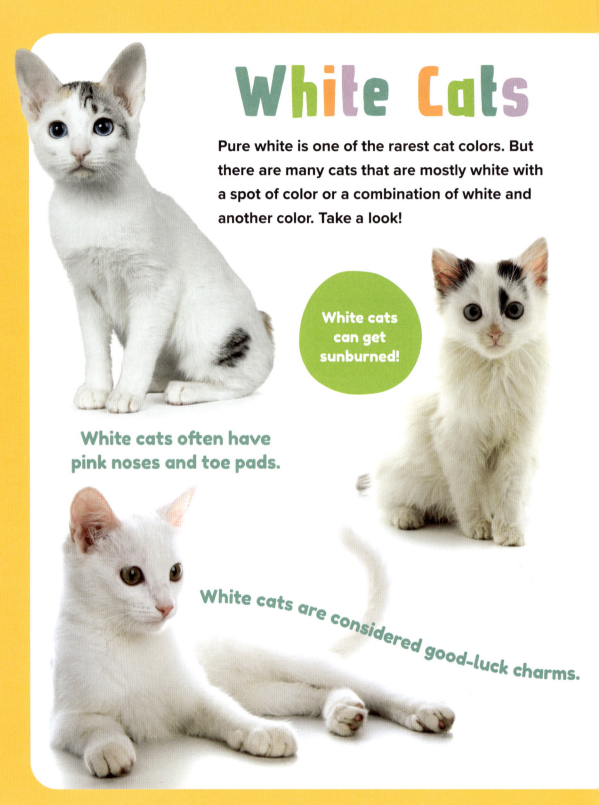

White cats can get sunburned!

White cats often have pink noses and toe pads.

White cats are considered good-luck charms.

Siamese

Persian

Many different breeds can be white.

White cats with blue eyes are often deaf.

Blue, green, yellow— white cats have different eye colors. Sometimes even more than one!

# WHAT IS THAT CAT SAYING?

Cats don't use words the way we do, but they have plenty to say if you listen. Here's how to understand what cats mean when they try to talk.

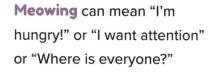

**Meowing** can mean "I'm hungry!" or "I want attention" or "Where is everyone?"

**Yowling** is a loud screeching sound that cats make when they are hurt, confused, or very angry.

**Purring** happens mostly when cats feel safe and happy, like when they snuggle with a favorite person. Sometimes cats purr when they're frightened, perhaps to comfort themselves.

Purr...

**Growling** means "Leave me alone!" This low, rumbling sound from the throat signals that a cat is protecting something or feels threatened.

Hiss!

Grrrr...

**Hissing** is a warning sign that a cat is frightened or angry.

# Fantastically Furry

Cat hair can be long and silky or thick and puffy. Most long-haired cats need frequent brushing to keep their coats from tangling or matting.

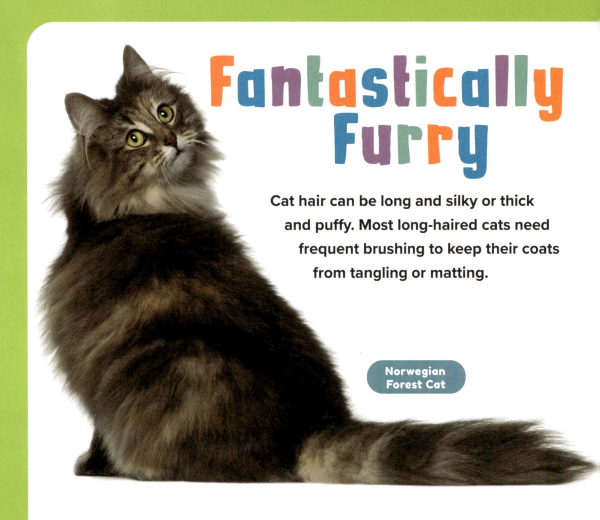

Norwegian Forest Cat

Cats can shed millions of hairs over their lifetime!

Persian

Sometimes cats swallow hair while they groom themselves.

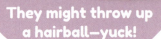

They might throw up a hairball—yuck!

Fur protects a cat's skin from cold, heat, and light. It also regulates body temperature.

British Longhair

Some long-haired cats have extra-hairy ears!

Domestic longhair

Most long-haired cats have a layer of fluffy fur next to their skin.

Maine Coon

Ragdoll

21

# Short Coats

Some cats have coats of fur that are smooth and sleek. Petting them is like petting velvet!

**The Sphinx is almost completely hairless.**

Some people who are allergic to cats can be around ones with short fur.

Sphinx

*The sleek Bengal has spots like a leopard.*

Bengal

Short-haired cats do shed, but not as much as long-haired ones.

Abyssinian

Some short coats are curly.

Devon Rex

The Korat is always silvery blue with no markings.

Korat

# All About Whiskers

Whiskers help cats figure out what's going on around them. Cats use them to find their way in the dark and to sense the presence of prey.

Cats have whiskers above their eyes, like our eyebrows.

Whiskers are much thicker than hairs.

Short whiskers on the front legs help cats find prey.

Cats prefer wide, shallow bowls so their whiskers don't get smushed while they eat or drink.

# Whisker Wonder

The position of a cat's whiskers can tell you how a cat is feeling.

Droopy whiskers indicate feeling relaxed.

**I'm curious!**

Whiskers pointing forward mean a cat is curious.

**I'm scared!**

Whiskers flattened to the face show that a cat feels scared or angry.

# Striped Cats

Striped cats are called tabbies. They can be gray, brown, or orange, with lots of thin stripes or a few wide ones.

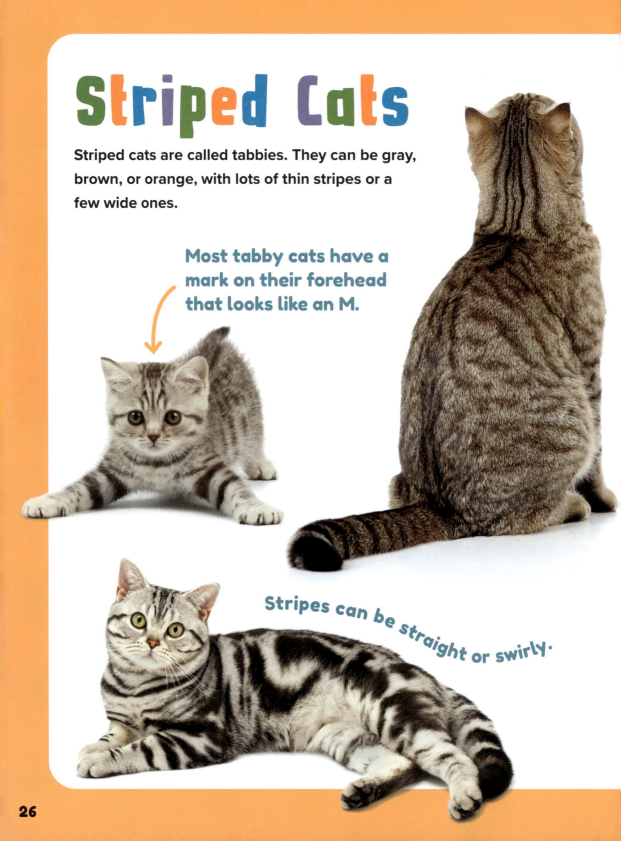

Most tabby cats have a mark on their forehead that looks like an M.

Stripes can be straight or swirly.

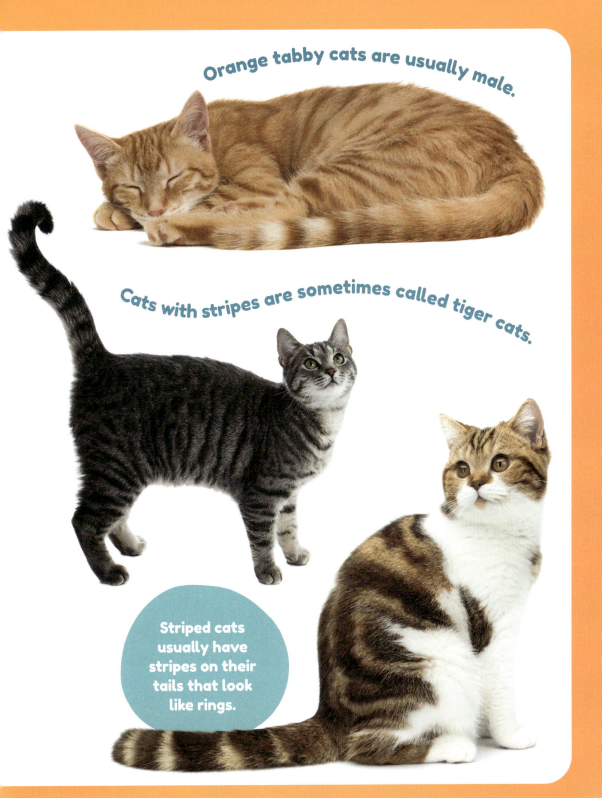

Orange tabby cats are usually male.

Cats with stripes are sometimes called tiger cats.

Striped cats usually have stripes on their tails that look like rings.

# HOW AM I LIKE A CAT?

In many ways, people and cats are alike. We are both mammals and have bones inside our bodies. We both have hair or fur, and our babies drink milk. But in other ways, cats and people are very different.

## Cat Superpowers

If you could pick one way to be more like a cat, what would it be? Do you wish you could jump five times your height? Would you like to have claws to climb and catch things with? Maybe it would be fun to have a tail and whiskers?

# CAT VS. PERSON

A side-by-side look at similarities and differences

## CAT  PERSON

 ### HAIR
Cats are covered with fur. People have lots of hair on their heads and a little on their bodies.

 ### CLAWS
Cats have claws that extend to catch prey. People have nails that protect their fingertips.

 ### EARS
Cats can move their ears around to hear where sounds are coming from. Humans can't do that!

 ### TONGUE
Cats clean themselves with their tongues. Humans take baths.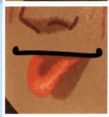

 ### TAIL
Cats have tails. Humans don't have tails.

 ### EYES
Feline pupils look like narrow slits. Human pupils are round.

# Paws and Claws

**Most cats have 18 toes. They have 5 on each front foot and 4 on each back foot. Their toes and the bottom of their paws are covered in thick skin instead of fur.**

claw

toe pad

metacarpal

**dewclaw**
A fifth toe, called the dewclaw, is higher up on the leg than the other four toes.

**whiskers**

Cats have sweat glands in their paws to help them cool off. They also have scent glands that leave an odor when they sharpen their claws.

A happy cat sitting on your lap might push its paws in and out. This is sometimes called "making biscuits" because it looks like they're kneading dough!

# How Claws Work

Cat claws stay hidden in their paws most of the time. But what happens when a cat wants to catch a mouse or scratch a post? Then the cat pushes the claws forward to expose the sharp tips.

Cats scratch to keep their claws sharp. A scratching post is better for that than a sofa!

Cats with more than five toes are called **POLYDACTYLS** (PAW-lee-DAK-tihls).

# Purebred Cats

Some cats are a particular breed, which means they belong to a group of cats that look alike. Have you seen any of these cat breeds?

Siamese

There are shows for purebred cats, where they can win ribbons for their looks.

Siamese cats have dark "points" on their faces, ears, legs, and tails.

Norwegian Forest Cat

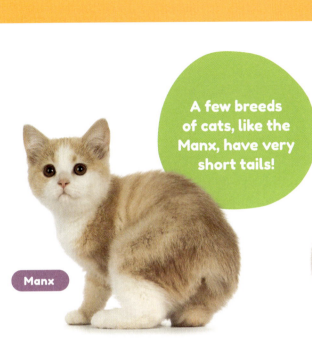

**Manx**

A few breeds of cats, like the Manx, have very short tails!

**Scottish Fold**

The LaPerm is named for its curly coat, a rare trait in cats.

**LaPerm**

**Sphinx**

33

# All About Ears

Cats have amazing hearing! When you meet a cat, notice the shape, size, and color of its ears, and look for the hair and veins.

Folded

Tufted

Veins

Orange

Small

Big

# Ear Talk

Cats have about 20 muscles in each ear! They can move their ears in many directions—and move each ear independently. Watch a cat's ears for clues to see how she's feeling.

A cat with ears up and pointed forward is alert and focused on something that interests or worries him.

With ears pressed flat and back, this cat is feeling nervous or scared.

Relaxed ears mean that a cat is feeling comfortable.

35

# Wild Cats

Have you seen lions, tigers, leopards, or other big cats at a zoo? As big as they are, they are related to our pet cats.

Tigers have webbed toes and like to swim.

Tiger

Cheetahs can run very fast in short bursts.

Lynx

Cheetah

# All About Eyes

All cats are born with blue eyes, but that color usually changes to gold, green, or brown as the cat grows. Feline eyes come in three shapes: round, almond, or slanted.

Blue

Gold

Green

Two colors

Wide pupil

Narrow pupil

# Taking a Catnap

Cats take lots of naps. So many naps, in fact, that they may sleep up to 18 hours a day! They will sleep almost anywhere, but often choose small spaces where they feel safe.

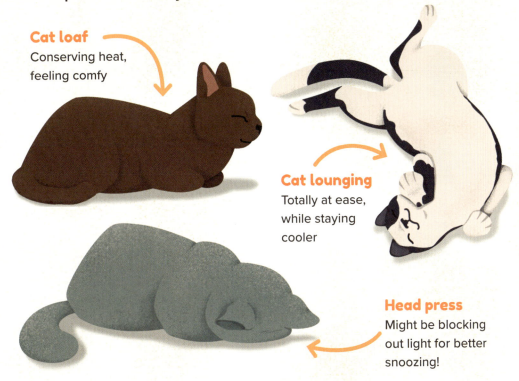

**Cat loaf**
Conserving heat, feeling comfy

**Cat lounging**
Totally at ease, while staying cooler

**Head press**
Might be blocking out light for better snoozing!

# Eye Facts

**Cats See Few Colors**
Cats can see yellow-green colors but have a harder time seeing shades of red.

**Cat Eyes Glow in the Dark**
Cats see in the dark better than we do. A reflective layer at the back of their eyes makes their eyes glow in the dark.

**Cats See Moving Objects**
Cats are better than we are at detecting rapid motion, like mice scurrying across the room!

# Cardboard Cat Toys

Cats love to pounce and play with toys. Here are some simple toys you can make out of a cardboard toilet-paper tube.

## Cardboard Ring

Cut a toilet-paper tube into rings. Cut fringe along both edges of each ring. Bend the fringe so it sticks out. Add some decoration, if you wish.

Toss these toys to your cat and see what it does with them!

# Catnip Toy

Slide a toilet-paper tube inside a sock. Add ½ cup dried catnip. Tie the loose end of the sock into a knot.

**Most cats love the smell of catnip!**

# Treat Toy

Cut a couple of small holes in a toilet-paper tube, a little larger than a cat treat. Fold down one end of the tube. Add a few treats and fold down the other end. Your cat will have fun batting the toy around to get the treats to fall out.

# BE KIND AND PLAY NICE

Cats tend to be a little shyer than dogs, but if you are patient, you can make friends with most cats. Here are some ways to let a cat know that you can be trusted to play nice.

**Speak quietly.** Cats can hear you even if you're whispering. Shouting and squealing can be frightening.

**Move slowly.** If you rush toward a cat, she might think you are going to hurt her and will run away.

### Use a favorite toy.
Ask the owner what the cat likes to play with. Some cats chase string, others like soft toys.

### Don't hold on!
Many cats don't like to be picked up or held, even by people they know. If a cat wants to be petted, sit next to him and pet gently.

**Be patient.** Try not to be sad or mad if a cat isn't in the mood to play. Maybe you could draw a picture of her instead!

**Be caring.** Treat cats with kindness and respect, just as you would like to be treated.

# Colorful Cats

One of the most fun and interesting things about cats is that they come in so many different colors. They have an amazing variety of patterns and color combinations.

Most tortoiseshell and calico cats are female.

Long-haired tortoiseshell

Short-haired tortoiseshell

Have you seen any unusual face colors?

Calico is a pattern of black, orange, and white. Each calico is different!

Calico

Orange and white

Spotted

Calico

## What a Character

Some people say that orange cats are friendly, gray cats are shy, and tabby cats are active. Sometimes that's true, but all cats have their own personalities!

# CATS IN MOTION

Cats may sleep a lot, but when they are active, they can really move! With their flexible bodies, paws with claws, and excellent sense of balance, cats love to run, jump, climb, and even swim.

Cats can jump up to five times their own height. That's like a person jumping as high as a house!

Cats use their tails to help keep their balance.

After climbing high, a cat must turn around and come down backward.

Have you ever seen a cat twist and turn in midair? They almost always land on their feet.

Most cats don't like to get wet, but the Turkish Van is a breed known as "the swimming cat."

A mother cat moves her kittens to safety by carrying them in her mouth.

47

# Kitty Kindness

If you love cats, you can help them by collecting items for an animal shelter that takes care of cats who need homes. When you visit the shelter to make your donation, you might get to meet some friendly cats!

Here are some things that shelters can use:

- Cat toys
- Beds
- Canned and dry food
- Cat treats
- Old towels and blankets
- Laundry detergent
- Paper towels
- Bleach

## Foster a Litter

**Some shelters look for families to foster a litter of kittens for a few weeks. Find out if you can sign up to do that. It's a fun way to learn about cats without owning one.**

# Cat Scavenger Hunt

Add a sticker to every green cat outline you see in this picture.

## LOOK FOR:

- A cat sitting in a window
- A cat playing with a toy
- A sleeping cat
- A cat licking its fur
- A cat pouncing
- A cat scratching
- A cat with its tail up
- A cat stretching
- A cat jumping
- A cat talking
- A cat eating

# I  CATS JOURNAL

### Keep a list of the cats you meet.

Name _____

Behavior _____

Color _____

Favorite toy _____

**WHY I LOVE THIS CAT:**

Name _____

Behavior _____

Color _____

Favorite toy _____

**WHY I LOVE THIS CAT:**

Name _____

Behavior _____

Color _____

Favorite toy _____

**WHY I LOVE THIS CAT:**

Name _____

Behavior _____

Color _____

Favorite toy _____

**WHY I LOVE THIS CAT:**

**The mission of Storey Publishing is to serve our customers by publishing practical information that encourages personal independence in harmony with the environment.**

**Edited by** Carleen Madigan and Lisa H. Hiley
**Art direction and book design by** Erin Dawson
**Text production by** Jennifer Jepson Smith

**Cover and interior illustrations** © Ivo Bordenave, DGPH studio (direction by Diego Vaisberg)/Advocate Art, Inc.
**Front cover photography by** © Nynke van Holten/Shutterstock.com, l.; © Oksana Kuzmina/Shutterstock.com, t.r.; © Peter Wollinga/Shutterstock.com, c.; © Utekhina Anna/Shutterstock.com, b.r.

**Interior photography by** © adogslifephoto/iStock.com, 8 b.r.; © Agency Animal Picture/Getty Images, 14 spotted; © Aleksey Mnogosmyslov/Shutterstock.com, 38 b.l.; © Anadolu/Getty Images, 47 m.r.; © Anatoliy Lukich/Shutterstock.com, 46 b.l.; © Anna Averianova/Shutterstock.com, 24 main; © Anton27/Shutterstock.com, 28; © Arina_B/Shutterstock.com, 21 t.; © Bianca Grueneberg/Shutterstock.com, 45 b.; © Chepko Danil Vitalevich/Shutterstock.com, 44 b.r.; © ChocoPie/Shutterstock.com, 34 t.l.; © COBRASoft/Shutterstock.com, 46 b.r.; © cynoclub/iStock.com, 20 b.l.; © Denis508/Shutterstock.com, 38 m.r.; © DenisNata/Shutterstock.com, 34 t.r.; © Dixi_/iStock.com, 10; © Dmitriy Krasko/Shutterstock.com, 47 t.; © Dorottya Mathe/Shutterstock.com, 14 feathery; © Dr.Margorius/Shutterstock.com, 1 t.l.; © Dzha33/Shutterstock.com, 27 b.; © E LLL/Shutterstock.com, 32 b.; © Ekaterina79/iStock.com, 34 m.r.; © Elena Zaretskaya/Getty Images, 19 t.; © Eric Isselee/Shutterstock.com, 5 r., 8 b.l., 17 t.l., 20 t., 33 t.r., 36, 37, 47 b.; © Ermolaev Alexander/Shutterstock.com, 9 b.r.; © Evgeniia Trushkova/Shutterstock.com, ii; © feedough/123RF.com, 5 b.l.; © fotogiunta/Shutterstock.com, 17 t.r.; © Gladkova Svetlana/Shutterstock.com, 22 t., 33 b.r.; © Happy monkey/Shutterstock.com, 6–7 all but 2 weeks; © Iakovleva Daria/Shutterstock.com, 44 b.l.; © Jagodka/Shutterstock.com, 17 b.; © Jane Koshchina/Shutterstock.com, 46 t.; © John Crowe/Alamy Stock Photo, 20 b.r.; © Jozefina777/Shutterstock.com, 8 t.; © Kasefoto/Shutterstock.com, 23 t.; © KDdesign_photo_video/Shutterstock.com, 38 t.l.; © Kirill Vorobyev/Shutterstock.com, 26 t.l.; © Kuttelvaserova Stuchelova/Shutterstock.com, 27 m.; © Kwanbenz/Shutterstock.com, 14 stubby; © Lena Miava/Shutterstock.com, 27 t.; © Litvalifa/Shutterstock.com, 16 m.; © Lux Blue/Shutterstock.com, 31 b.; © M_Light/Shutterstock.com, 38 m.l.; © Margarita Borodina/Shutterstock.com, 23 m.; Mars Vilaubi © Storey Publishing, 40–41; © MirasWonderland/Shutterstock.com, 1 b.r.; © MOLPIX/Shutterstock.com, 12 b.l.; © MyImages - Micha/Shutterstock.com, 31 m.; © Nikita Rublev/Shutterstock.com, 13 l.; © Nils Jacobi/Shutterstock.com, 34 b.l.; © NiseriN/iStock.com, 9 t.r.; © Norman Chan/Shutterstock.com, 5 t.; © Nynke van Holten/Shutterstock.com, 1 t.r., 16 t., 21 b.l., 23 b., 32 t., 33 b.l. & t.l., 45 t.l. & t.r.; © Oksana Kuzmina/Shutterstock.com, 1 b.l., 26 t.r.; © Olezzo/Shutterstock.com, 21 c.; © Pixel-Shot/Shutterstock.com, 13 t.; © PokoFoto/Shutterstock.com, 18 t.; © Pressmaster/Shutterstock.com, 16 b.; © Reggie Barroga/Shutterstock.com, 9 b.l.; © Ruslan Shugushev/Shutterstock.com, 6 2 weeks; © schankz/Shutterstock.com, 14 curled; © Seregraff/Shutterstock.com, 22 b., 34 b.r., 44 t.; © Sharomka/Shutterstock.com, 18 b.; © Slava Dumchev/Shutterstock.com, 19 b.r.; © Sonsedska Yuliia/Shutterstock.com, 30; © StockPhotosArt/Shutterstock.com, 13 r.; © theksu/Shutterstock.com, 38 b.r.; © Tony Campbell/Shutterstock.com, 4 t., 9 t.l., 13 b.r.; © TungCheung/Shutterstock.com, 14 colorful; © Utekhina Anna/Shutterstock.com, 12 b.r.; © Valeri Luzina/Shutterstock.com, 19 b.l.; © vector owl/Shutterstock.com, 38 t.r.; © Viktor Lugovskoy/Shutterstock.com, 24 inset; © Viorel Sima/Shutterstock.com, 12 t.r.; © Vivienstock/Shutterstock.com, 45 m.r.; © vkbhat/iStock.com, 4 b.; © Vladyslav Starozhylov/Shutterstock.com, 26 b.; © Yaya Photos/Shutterstock.com, 34 m.l.; © YULIYA Shustik/Shutterstock.com, 31 t.; © Yuliya/iStock.com, 14 striped; © Zharinova Marina/Shutterstock.com, 21 b.r.

Text © 2025 by Storey Publishing

All rights reserved. Hachette Book Group supports the right to free expression and the value of copyright. The purpose of copyright is to encourage writers and artists to produce the creative works that enrich our culture. The scanning, uploading, and distribution of this book without permission is a theft of the author's intellectual property. If you would like permission to use material from the book (other than for review purposes), please contact permissions@hbgusa.com. Thank you for your support of the author's rights.

The information in this book is true and complete to the best of our knowledge. All recommendations are made without guarantee on the part of the author or Storey Publishing. The author and publisher disclaim any liability in connection with the use of this information.

The publisher is not responsible for websites (or their content) that are not owned by the publisher.

Storey books may be purchased in bulk for business, educational, or promotional use. Special editions or book excerpts can also be created to specification. For details, please contact your local bookseller or the Hachette Book Group Special Markets Department at special.markets@hbgusa.com.

**Storey Publishing**
210 MASS MoCA Way
North Adams, MA 01247
storey.com

Storey Publishing is an imprint of Workman Publishing, a division of Hachette Book Group, Inc., 1290 Avenue of the Americas, New York, NY 10104. The Storey Publishing name and logo are registered trademarks of Hachette Book Group, Inc.

Distributed in Europe by Hachette Livre, 58 rue Jean Bleuzen, 92 178 Vanves Cedex, France
Distributed in the United Kingdom by Hachette Book Group, UK, Carmelite House, 50 Victoria Embankment, London EC4Y 0DZ

ISBNs: 978-1-63586-920-0 (paper over board with 2 sticker sheets and fold-out journal); 978-1-63586-921-7 (fixed format EPUB); 978-1-63586-974-3 (fixed format PDF); 978-1-63586-975-0 (fixed format Kindle)

Printed in Humen Town, Dongguan, China by R. R. Donnelley on paper from responsible sources
10 9 8 7 6 5 4 3 2 1

APS
November 2024

# Play, Learn & Have Fun
## with These Other Storey Books

 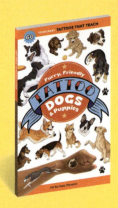 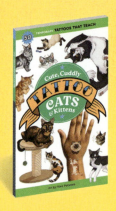

### Animal Friends: Hello, Dogs!

This photo-packed book, perfect for dog-crazy kids ages 4 and up, tells about the various breeds and types of dogs; how dogs see, hear, and communicate; what makes them happy; how to make friends with them; and much more. Includes 50 stickers!

### Furry, Friendly Tattoo Dogs & Puppies

Kids will love these 60 temporary tattoos, which include favorite breeds, playful poses, and irresistibly cute puppies. The tattoos are easy to apply and last up to a week.

### Cute, Cuddly Tattoo Cats & Kittens

These 50 easy-to-apply temporary tattoos are absolutely adorable and last up to a week. A perfect gift for cat-loving kids!

**Join the conversation.** Share your experience with this book, learn more about Storey Publishing's authors, and read original essays and book excerpts at storey.com. Look for our books wherever quality books are sold or call 800-441-5700.